Helen of Troy, 1993

Poems

Maria Zoccola

Scribner

New York   Amsterdam/Antwerp   London   Toronto   Sydney   New Delhi

Scribner
An Imprint of Simon & Schuster, LLC
1230 Avenue of the Americas
New York, NY 10020

First Scribner trade paperback edition January 2025

SCRIBNER and design are trademarks of Simon & Schuster, LLC

For information about special discounts for bulk purchases,
please contact Simon & Schuster Special Sales at 1-866-506-1949
or business@simonandschuster.com.

The Simon & Schuster Speakers Bureau can bring authors to your live event.
For more information or to book an event, contact the Simon & Schuster Speakers Bureau at 1-866-248-3049 or visit our website at www.simonspeakers.com.

Interior design by Davina Mock-Maniscalco

Manufactured in the United States of America

10 9 8 7 6 5 4 3 2 1

Library of Congress Cataloging-in-Publication Data

Names: Zoccola, Maria, 1993– author.
Title: Helen of Troy, 1993 : poems / Maria Zoccola.
Description: First Scribner trade paperback edition. | New York : Scribner, 2025.
Identifiers: LCCN 2024012302 (print) | LCCN 2024012303 (ebook) |
  ISBN 9781668046333 (trade paperback) | ISBN 9781668046340 (ebook)
Subjects: LCSH: Helen, of Troy, Queen of Sparta—Poetry. | LCGFT: Poetry.
Classification: LCC PS3626.O28 H45 2025 (print) | LCC PS3626.O28 (ebook) |
  DDC 811/.6—dc23/eng/20240418
LC record available at https://lccn.loc.gov/2024012302
LC ebook record available at https://lccn.loc.gov/2024012303

ISBN 978-1-6680-4633-3
ISBN 978-1-6680-4634-0 (ebook)

She thinks, part woman, three parts a child,
That nobody looks; her feet
Practise a tinker shuffle
Picked up on the street.

—"Long-Legged Fly," W. B. Yeats

There was a world... or was it all a dream?

—*Iliad* 3.219, tr. Robert Fagles

Contents

Family Tree, 1993

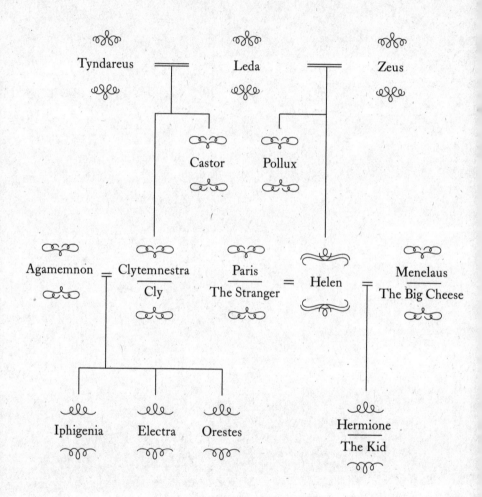

Helen of Troy,
1993

helen of troy feuds with the neighborhood

if you never owned a bone-sharp biography,
i don't want to hear it. if you didn't slide
from the house at night to roll 4-wheelers
out the shed, if you didn't catch branches
on your cheeks and flip the beast
in a mud rut, go down yelling, come up
laughing, if you didn't roar the woods
with star-love brothers, with blood-wait sister,
squinting through pine dirt, through cobweb,
through creatures with fur that explode
into wings, through devils with fins
that grow legs and run. through boys
who become brutes and become boys again.
through girls who die
and stay that way. if you didn't see a swan
become a wolf. if you didn't see a wolf
clamp teeth around a swan. if you didn't
go away and come back again,
helen judas, helen stranger, trojan helen,
helen of the outside. if you didn't limp
your way home, dark house, door sealed tight,
all the street with eyes sewn shut,
i don't want to hear it. i want you silent.
i want you listening to me.

Sparta, Tennessee

AD 1993

helen of troy makes an entrance

i was born from the shell of an egg my mother pushed
from between her thighs, crouched on her hospital bed
like a woman beating slips against a river rock, hollering
for the nurse, for the gyno trapped down the hall
with breech twins, for the state of tennessee to pull off
its work gloves and hold her hand. a mottled blue crowning.
sheets stained and stinking. there was enough time,
before the cracks began, to hold the egg in her arms,
put her cheek to the smooth wall, still warm and wet
from her body. she told me it was as if she held a kind
of anchorage, of holy cell, and to her ears there came
a humming that kept its meter and kept its rhyme,
and my mother, poor woman, knew enough to fear
a daughter birthed to song. herself and her own shelled child,
rocking gently to the box fan's moan. past the window
were realms of corrugated steel, scrub trees huddled
in roadside ditches, the far-off nuclear plant that might
maybe blow, might maybe save us all. a state of being
she could never recreate: i was outside her body and yet
i was safe, hidden, seen by none but amniotic flowers,
my name a byword for hot closed shield. how to stop a story
from spinning itself to completion? how to arrest a world
in its own natal dark? the quill is scratching. you can hear it,
can't you: a sound like the tapping of an egg-tooth.
like ice beneath a dancer's heel. mother, they're coming,
the ward to your door. they'll bathe me, dress me,
certify my skin. they'll wrap me in blankets
of pre-woven thread, cut and tied long before
i breathed the wash of hospital air. let them, mother.
give them my name. let them pass it back and forth
like builders who raise a chamber in lines of stone.

helen of troy calls her sister

cly, you remember when it was us and the boys
and mom and dad and we all drove up
to chincoteague for the summer and the car just—
collapsed—
just broke down, and dad took the hood up
and put his head in the engine and hollered
for mom to keep turning the key and the sky—
like fire—
record heat, air-con kaput with the rest
and the sun crushing down like a mouthful
of lemon peels, like the inside of a deer's gut—
and castor—
wouldn't get out of the car, he was afraid
of the snakes, you remember the snakes,
buckets of them wiggling around the trees—
rising up—
leaping up to strike, and i said momma don't
you see what's happening, but that's when dad
all punked on motor oil snatched up a rock—
a boulder—
biggest one he could find, and he smashed
that thing down on the engine so hard i thought
the earth had split, sound like a plane crash—
like a death—
but damned if that engine didn't roll right
over for him, just spread its legs and purred,
and there was nothing sweeter than pulling out—
past the trucks—
past the men, none of whom had stopped
to help, and castor, poor kid, didn't he throw up?
all over the back seat, smelled like milk and rot—

all the way to virginia—

       all the way to the big house, you remember
       the hurricane? you remember the hydrangeas,
       how they looked so bright inside the storm?

helen of troy in february

do i love him? who, the big cheese?
enough to be stood here in this walgreens
with his gut pills in my purse and the baby
slung on my chest, with bing crosby
piped through the speakers and the slip-choke
of pink and red and puff snowed in
on every shelf, cards like you wouldn't
believe, my honey bear, my shining star.
his name's on the mortgage.
on the title to the car. at night he says
what did you do today helen and listens,
i mean really listens, when i say
well i changed the baby and took the car
through the wash, all those words
straight and tidy, little soldiers
on the march, my mouth to that baking
marsh of his insides where crooked
things lie down and begin to sink.
i give him   arrows. my lover,
hearts and kisses, silk petals
in the centerfold, one ninety-nine
before tax. envelope like fogged
glass. line at the register snaking
nearly to the exit sign, where sliding
doors roar open to the snow.

the spartan women discuss the local waterfowl

beautiful and suffering from a mortal wound,
the swan chooses our boat ramp for her death
song. our mothers warned us this could happen:
a creature, past the point of endurance,
becomes in extremis a lantern of heaven.
some hurts, set to music, drown themselves
before the chorus. others deconstruct
into gristle and breath, a town bleaching
in the flare of a handful of brilliant lives.
we're frozen on the riverbank, pinned by
a sound that could crack our foundations,
that could transform us, unless we stop it cold.
our children run to touch what is dying—
their fathers, of course, are upstream with the guns.

helen of troy's new whirlpool washing machine

well she cost about a pig and a half but the old girl was sending up the most pulverizing full-body shakes whenever i loaded her down with more than just a nightie and the kid's school duds—whole blessèd homestead brought to a standstill lord i never knew such a house for turning out dirty laundry—and i said to the big cheese i said to him *not one more evening arm-deep in drum scum not another night blind-fishing for long johns* and boy was i ever building up to a real snitty fit-pitching or worse a one-wife washerwoman picket line *and then who would suds my drawers* no doubt his heart cried out in tones of both humility and contrition since sears & roebuck blazed down the street double quick to black-bag broke betsy and wizard up a machine straight from the cave of wonders i mean factory *fresh* six cycles two speeds spin like a star trek thingamajig *is it good enough for you helen* what a thing to ask as if i don't crank the dial ten times a day just to watch the foam and when she really gets up and running doesn't she just suck out the stains—

about the affair

from my place in his bed, the trees in the side yard
burst into red and gold beacons
as if some nymph or muse pulled them leaf by leaf
from the hot folds of her body.
it was always this way, for me. the blazing went on
until the dark came, and the dark went on
for much longer than that.

helen of troy is asked to the spring formal

every bird in the sky begged to be my man. each worm in the dirt longed to wife me. when i swam in shallow creeks, leeches encircled my ring finger in black bands. i shimmered with a magic of hair or ankle, some perfection of sex that bent to my neck in powdered down, cutex-sharp at nails and toes, coats of flashing fuchsia frost. rats swarmed from their roofly nests. deer massed in the leaves before my blind, and then came the boys, pickup trucks and heavy bass, paper cups to hold brown spit. they snarled and swore and muddied the lawn, they bloodied the lawn, they held each other and rutted in the lawn, sun-scald sweating them dry, undershirts yanked off, rivers of skin like the milk of my own hunger. i took their gifts. i counted them: dolly on vinyl, dolly on cassette, remington bolt-actions and tripods of gold, mud-covered jeeps with half-paid notes, a basket of rags with a cygnet inside. they offered themselves, their mothers' farms, their fathers' bread, their bodies new-spun from childhood clay. *come down to us*, they howled to my window. *we'll pelt you like the forest fox. we'll strip you clean, we'll lick you raw. you'll see why trees lie down for the axe.* i listened. i went. i never came back.

(interlude: the swan describes the next hour)

she's sitting on the tub edge, which is across from the sink. the mirror comes down a long way, so even while she's sitting she can see how her hair is tangled around her ears and the crown of her head. she's waiting for the thing that's coming, the slow creep of movement over the skin, like standing in a puddle with long jeans, feeling the damp climb higher by degrees. she thinks she will be able to see the change in the mirror in the bathroom, and then later in the mirror in the bedroom, and later still in the dark glass of storefronts and car windows, the places she walks out in the world among people who might now know her for one of their own, or else for a foreigner come among them by hidden means. but she's wrong; there is no change. she is exactly the same, except for the tangled hair and the marks along her hips where he bruised her, even though he tried not to.

helen of troy tells her mother it's a graduation girls' trip and drives alone to the clinic in nashville

the secret to the hair is backcombing till your arms go numb,
long shank locked between forefinger and thumb, snarls
of bottle blond shaved down on a comb as spry and quick
as the scraps lit before each football game, the boys jumpy
with nerves, savaging each other in short growling bursts.
this is after the hot rollers, before the aqua net, chemical fog
floating through the motel 6, catching on the mirror, the faucet,
the light bulb, the back of your throat when you huff down
the burn. eyes in baby blue, lined with black pencil,
swoop the sides out and up, powder, brow tint, two coats
of mascara. lipliner in coral glow, filler a blend of covergirl
and maybelline. cosmo propped against the hair dryer, may of '81:
i had a nose job and look at me now!, blush done up just like
kelly le brock. two spritzes to finish, neck and wrist,
rub the pulse points together, rose and lilac running wild,
an open field you can see when you unfocus your eyes,
what's that growing there, what is that harvest coming in,
gold upon gold, a sweet wind that takes the clouds and pushes
them higher, throws the birds into tumbled exclamation, oh—
keys in the purse. aspirin. two aspirin. final check: teeth, hair,
nails, eyes, dab the eyes, don't smudge, don't ruin it, not for
something so small, for one slip—after all that work.

the spartan women discuss the big cheese

still wading upstream with father and gun,
the boy studies fundamentals—desire
to acquisition, the chosen heart dragged
earthward to crater in pools of mud and silt.
proper stance requires perfect mimicry.
he'll be the hero of our story, you know,
this child pressed forward by a current
so gentle it might be a thread of silk
tied in loops to his first and second ribs.
soft tug, early morning, fingers slowly
numbing in the cold. he cuddles the gun
against his chest. his father's up ahead,
a stone around which the river must crack.
there are not ways of living. there's one way.

helen of troy meets the big cheese

as in the dampest part of winter, when rain
                    flushes down from a sky
with spring growing in its eye like a cataract
not yet thick enough to film,
wetting branches already spongy with snowmelt
and too old to bargain another year's sap
                    from the mother trunk,
and the wind blows with sudden exclamation
against the topmost bough,
                    and that bough tumbles down,
knocking here and there and falling square against
a second limb, snapping it from the tree,
and both limbs
                    —sopped with rot and soft with death—
drop together to the pine needle core of the forest floor
and lie one atop the other, unmoving and jointly locked,
decomposing by turns—just so
did i first lay eyes on him. just so did we begin.

helen of troy catalogues her pregnancy cravings

pickles. peanut butter off a spoon. that cereal
with the little blue guys on it, the gnome things in hats,
they have the cartoon where they're all men
except for that one blond babe who struts around
in white manolos and a flirty little slip
and all the blue guys beat each other to death over her,
a blue guy massacre, a real grisly piece of television,
although maybe i'm getting it mixed up
with something else, maybe i fell asleep watching it
and kind of dreamed the rest,
maybe what i'm really craving these days is
violence, or maybe it's still chocolate.
corn chips. sliced watermelon. microwave pizza rolls.
bags of gummy sharks. ice cream, like a *lot* of ice cream,
cartons of fudge ripple i pound in one sitting
with a spoon like a dirt mover, scoop scoop
down the hole, layers of white ounces plugged
right into the skin, who was that one wizard in salem
they squashed to death in a tofu press,
giles somebody, they just kept piling it on,
and that sucker smiled his bluebird smile
and asked for more. cheesecake. jelly rolls. i'm trying
to weigh myself down, and the kid's not doing it
fast enough. a house has to settle on its foundation,
has to stuff itself with so much life
there's no need to beg for more. triscuits, i tell him.
get me birdseed and eggshells and shards of ice.
i want to break something on my teeth. i want to crush
it so fine the load goes down like abracadabra,
alakazam, watch me make the whole thing disappear.

helen of troy in the delivery ward

one summer i took a job at a debt collector's—
answering calls and placing them, reading off a script:
here is the sum in precise decimals, here is a list
of the things we will take, here is a place you can go
to lay down jewelry, car titles, deeds to land
your father owned—eight hours of this, june and july,
every minute pushed into the red lick of self
that waited for breath to start again, cord coil
tattooing around my arms, spine anchored down
against the sounds feeding back to me across the line.
outside the hills pulsed with flycatchers and
medicine moths, weasels and the mice they stalked,
boys trapping out of season, the beasts that died
in their snares.   i banned my husband
from the hospital room. my body worked
a second shift, and it was no different, in fact,
from any other kind of work, any other moment
i closed the space inside my mind where i lived
and became a thing made of oil and rag, stripped
of all i owed, held down, picked clean. what is this
animal, i thought, at the end of it all. what is this
brick, what is this ringing phone?

helen of troy avoids her school reunion

a golden shovel from *Iliad* 6.408–409, tr. Robert Fagles

you start off all bowl-cut tube-sock schoolhouse rock and end up a bitch,
and i've never been able to clock when it happened, what fine day that
lemon soured, what burger i'd snarfed for lunch, what copy of tiger beat i
was caking in doodle hearts while the proclamation rang out: i was, i am,
i ever shall be, bitch-hood delivered by angels on high gumming vicious
wads of bubble yum and sliding each other these sweet little scheming
glances, as if i hadn't already tea-leaved my fate straight out of the horror
of the morning bus ride. their cherry-pie faces, of course i was gagging to
know: was it my hair, my clothes, was it the way i didn't good-girl freeze
when kevin smith touched my waist, the way i laughed and loosened the
buckled cage of my ribs, how i reached in right away to dig out my heart?

helen of troy cranks the volume on "like a prayer" in the ballet studio parking lot

listen, madonna, he's worth it like a box of hot krispy kremes is worth it,
six glazed cavity grenades pounded in the eight minutes it takes the kid
to finish gabbing with her dance-class kill squad and sling her way
into my passenger seat and no she *won't* take a jam-filled anything
because her plié overlord says it's time to lose the babyfat, babygirl,
so that's the rest of the box forsworn to the back bench while i
sticky-finger steer my way home unzipping my attention between
the road tonight's dinner my ingrown toenail gas prices at the texaco
how many weeks it's been since my last period and the pearls of gossip
from the kid on lila elise's mama who drank too much and had to go
to a special home in nashville so when i park and go inside and start
chopping onions for the pan of hot oil i guess i've forgotten all about
the crate of sugar sitting in the station wagon until three days later
when i pop open the side door to slide in some groceries and *scream*
because that's more ants than i've ever seen in my entire god-loving
life undulating across the seat covers in jet-black tv static to pick up
each crumb of sweetness and grind it into the corners and rips and
secret places so deep my whole life's gonna be ants and chocolate
whenever folks look at my face they're gonna see the smear
of a meal i ate when i was starving that was better in the gut than
let's say battery acid or the dead skin around my own manicure
but did not in the end make my belly stop howling did not in the end
keep the car in the drive.

helen of troy watches jurassic park in theaters

a month ago it was horses horses horses but the moon
turned and the kid was red-eye rabid on shovels and dirt
egyptology archaeology paleontology blitzed all to hell
on dead crap somebody stuck in a hole and forgot about
and then what should hit the local cineplex but dinosaurs
cavorting in dazzles of cgi glory i mean it was inescapable
t-rexes plastered on every bus bench from here to hosanna
and the kid threatening a hunger strike if i didn't bring her
opening night and then somehow the big cheese entered
the spirit of the thing but only i think because he got wind
of the carnage lurking within although naturally he didn't
give me the slightest whisper of warning until we were
an hour in and the tyrannosaur was snapping up its first
victim like the last ham cube at your cousin's baby shower
i mean blood *everywhere* and you know what i couldn't
look away it was a total saturday-night gore-fest and i
was *hooked* okay i was *invested* i was cheering that damn
lizard on while it chased down all those folks with their
miserable problems and unhappinesses and inane little
cruelties shared over the dinner table like it's amazing how
you spent thirty dollars on blue jeans instead of getting
the vacuum fixed it stomped them *flat* like good *night* like
sweet dreams and sayonara and it was a full eight minutes
before i noticed the kid was over there in total convulsions
of terror and dread all googly-eyed and weeping and i did
care i'm not a monster any other second i'd be right there
scooping her up and dashing for the lobby and hugging and
kissing and squeezing and so forth et cetera but right then
i wasn't me at all i wasn't mama i wasn't woman i wasn't
helen i was yellow teeth at night i was rip and tear and
mouth of blood i was something so large i shook the earth

unpennable unappeasable intractable i was this thing
no one would ever dare call beautiful and eventually it was
the big cheese who grabbed her up and shoved past me
down the aisle carrying our child to safety while onscreen
i roared and snapped and everyone around me bowed.

the spartan women discuss the family

there are not ways of living. there's one way
out of the mud and one way back in, if you're
concerned about that sort of thing. we're not.
our eyes are glued on the hereafter,
but also on which neighborhood sinners
have turned up for sunday service. we like
to take attendance, unofficially,
just a little whisper to share over coffee
in the church hall. there are some the night
squeezes and won't let go, and we need to know
what dirt to pray for. leda's clan, for one,
sweet people, four kids, in the pew each week,
all of them kneeling on a very thin board,
the empty place yawning open beneath them.

helen of troy gets the news from her sister

and now for the death report, shuffle-snap of newsprint staticking down the line,
background howl of kiddies brawling for froot loops and wielding skip-its like
morningstars, sharp shriek for each blooming bruise. *three boys in west memphis,*
seventy-six waco branch davidians, ten thousand under an earthquake in india,
are you listening to me, helen, a ferry sank in south korea and everyone on board
drowned. my sister before church, after golf, between rounds on the thighmaster:
'93 meant death in daily installments, plastic-wrapped reaper-man delivered
before dawn to the driveway's dirt dip, cly cradling the cordless in the soft
of her neck and shouting her three tax breaks into shoes and bags and bus—
or two tax breaks now, i should say, i must remember to say,
although we don't talk children, mine or hers, we talk car bombs and clinton
and an alabama amtrak run off the big bayou bridge, forty-seven dead,
and when we run out of black-and-white we turn on channel six to watch
charles gibson roll down the teleprompter and tell us how the srebrenican safe zone
is a beacon in the dark. some phone calls you know from the landline's first voice,
the augur of the bell a skinned nerve jamming the kitchen with noise,
one long night and the headline to follow, the quiet obit, the funeral, the wake,
the news delivered from mouth to mouth across bellsouth's web of silver wires,
an endless ringing i hear in my sleep. it's no wonder my sister can't stop calling,
we're bombing mogadishu, we're bombing baghdad, little tick marks on an internal
chalkboard, tiny weights added to a heart-held scale, a year of swallowing bylines
and vomiting them back out again, every hour a new scoop, names above the fold,
names below, her daughter a lede she buries with both hands.

(interlude: the swan describes the harvest)

they're bringing in the tobacco farther north, close to the kentucky
border, hacking it away from its roots by hand with small axes. the
tobacco plant is the size of a man, if you also hacked a man with
small axes and planted his torso in tilled-up earth. he is heavy. his
leaves drag the dirt like dark green lungs. workers drive his body
onto spikes and hang him in the rafters of smoking barns, ready to
be fired from below by burning piles of sawdust and board. once,
as a small child, helen saw a woman rush out to the center of a ripe
field and leap into the air, seven or eight feet high, the gods dragging
her upward by the scruff of her neck. it was not a tobacco field,
but later helen can't remember what crop was grown there, what
stalk cradled the woman when she fell. it might have been soy. there
are soy fields near her now, mounded up to the waist like rows of
low-crouched hounds, muscles straining, holding back. when the
yield is in, workers shut up the tobacco barns for weeks. pure white
smoke escapes from slats near the roof and drifts across the county.
the dispatcher's line rings over and over, strangers on the highway
convinced there's a fire, fearing someone is trapped, in danger.

helen of troy surfs the net

well listen okay the whole color classic starts heating up
like a goddamn fish skillet and making these hellacious
groaning sounds just caterwauling right there on the desk
beside the cookbooks and car keys and piles of the kid's
history flash cards and i'm thinking christ if this thing blows
it's taking half the kitchen down with it and the new oven
hardly with the shine off it yet so i'm scrambling through
notebooks and post-its and the backs of chi-chi's receipts
for wherever it was i thought to scratch down that help line
the one off computer chronicles of course you know
computer chronicles comes on pbs in the late nights
after the second run on charlie rose and what else
was i supposed to do, call the big cheese? his work line?
ring him up and say hey baby i'm fixing to set the house
on fire 'cause i can't get along with your new macintosh?
and to tell you the truth i'm not even supposed to be
touching the thing not even meant to be looking at it
on account of all the folks you can meet online these days
all those weirdos who sit around on message boards
just waiting to lend an ear to some sweet thing who can't
stand one more half hour of driving the dress shirts
to the dry cleaner and buffing the goddamn naugahyde,
who might take a peek at my shapely megabytes
and say oh you poor honey why don't i send you a one-way
plane ticket right out to my castle in beverly hills or
san francisco and that would be *that* i swear to christ
although he didn't use quite those exact words
when he explained to me why i should keep my paws
off the keyboard (the big cheese i mean). so there i am
strangling myself with the phone cord punching in numbers
and blasting my own ear with a sewer pipe of feedback

like somebody's deboning a xylophone because i guess
i've somehow managed to fire up the internet after all
and then all at once the whole heap shudders and coughs
and flatlines, just real-as-life bites the big one, death-wail
and a pitch-black screen and i'm left crouched in my chair
with one grip on the phone and the other crushed down so hard
on my own thigh i feel the flab squish like play-doh, whole
house quiet as a tick bite, one more escape hatch gone dark.

another thing about the affair

i thought the elm would croak if we kept burying
any more of the kid's dead fish in the roots,
orange cyanide from the fair, lived long enough
for me to bag the whole kit at fin world, bowl and gravel
and flakes in a jar, then belly-up, all of them—like *that*.
don't ask me about it, cly.
there was a morning when the kid stormed the bus
and vanished, twenty faces in those grimy windows
and i couldn't pick hers out, her hair the same
as everyone else's hair and her face the same
as everyone else's face and some of those hands were hers
but i couldn't tell which ones, craning my neck
on the curb in my housecoat and snow boots, absolutely killing myself
to find this girl who's suddenly like rubber
in my mind, like a baby doll stripped down
to blank skin, and you know what i guess i really did just
stop trying, and when the bus pulled off and left me all alone
on the street with the skeleton trees and buried
lawns and dead fish lurking below the crust,
didn't i just stop trying
on everything else.

helen of troy folds laundry in a dim room

i don't know if you have ever started growing
away from yourself.
                    a ribbed shuck peeled down,
inch by inch, from the gold. shadows on the dirt:
corn bending toward the harvester, leaning forward
                    in relief.

helen of troy runs the station wagon into a ditch

you ever get going down a long stretch of some
county road way out in the sticks where nobody
knows your name or your people or just exactly
how many babies you did or did not have
and what happened to them afterward?
sun full in your face. fm station coming in glassy
as a jar of night cream. and why shouldn't you
speed up? and why shouldn't your toes itch
on that pedal so sweet and easy you might as well
be that sugar from the movies? be that doll
from the papers, hanging off the battlements,
teeth sharper than a hairpin turn? velocity,
transmutation, oh baby, that arc through
the wind, that barrel roll, they shoulda been here
with the cameras, me and me in black and white,
blasted down the line for the world to skin up
over morning coffee, fingers rolling down
the page, my name typed up where it can't
blow away again. the kind of thing you clip
for the scrapbook. the kind of girl you save.

helen of troy recovers at st. francis

what a fuss, this phalanx of nurses,
these meals in brown plastic, lettuce and ham.
bones in a cast, cast in a sling. bandages
sticking my scalp back together.
that mirror in the bathroom, red ghost,
some sweet creature ripped along
and away. i touch my wild hair,
come away with shards of glass
the women missed. night machines
like marching men, and then, at dawn,
the child in gray scrubs, her clipboard
and pen. she wants me to say
i lost control. her poor twitching knee,
her glance at the door.

helen of troy cleans up after the barbecue

smoke rose from the cooling grill in inconstant streams,
at times hazing around the mounted floodlight, at times indistinguishable
from the envelope of night. wild things from the woods
treated our home as their home, stealing among the sinks and rises
of the land my husband owned and making off
with what they found there; the fence, nearly finished, was new.
stars burrowed across a wool shroud, wet lines of vapor
tracking headlights in the road. i was bending at the knees
and rising again, gathering the white plates
from their separate pools of darkness, bringing them up
from cool and ant-filled grass. i didn't know i was a person
until i stopped being one. my mind held this thought only distantly
as i worked, the way a dog barking far-off
becomes to the ear a kind of metallic ringing.
the white plates glowed like scattered moons; i could choose
which one to kneel to next. hinges like birdcall:
the screen door slapping against its frame. my husband
on the patio, returning chairs to their ordered line.
it was early fall. the trees were changing, but the air still burned.
i wore nothing on my arms. neither did he.

and another thing about the affair

the next guest on good morning america was a hypnotist.
he had a live studio audience and a girl who seemed
tied to her chair by something stronger than chain, a girl
who carried in her perfect teeth—how did i know—
a species of yellow poison.
i'd never seen it happen, the pocket watch on its chain,
the white bar of intention welding two creatures together,
you are getting very sleepy, how her mouth went

                                                    slack.
yeah, like that. our hands met and the watch started ticking,
pendulum swing of minutes swirling a black drain, the cuff
on his sleeve undone by one button, the way he smelled
like something moving far-off.
i followed him to his car. how did i know, how did the world
form a tunnel with this star at its mouth? the asphalt roared open.
birds in the air turned away from our path. who was it who said
            the words, who asked the final question?
if i can just grip the edges of it. if i can close my fist and catch
the blade on the inside. ghost-helen, helen made of mist
and light, who ran and ate and returned my body when
the stage went dark.
if i could shake myself awake, i don't think i'd try.
good morning tennessee! when the great zirconi snaps
his fingers, you'll find yourself unrecognizable. you'll find
yourself of renamed genus, carbon altered, built for land
that's not your own.

the spartan women discuss tennessee

ten thousand empty places yawn open
beneath our turf, more bubbles of dead air
than any other state. that's a fact
the babies read in school, the size of the land
beneath the land. what's been found inside.
on spelunking tours, there's a moment the guide
turns off her lamp. we learn that darkness
is an animal like us, silken
and hungry, heavy as a child
too old to be carried, an amorphous host
of mortal fear. relit, the lamp guides us
down a staircase clawed into the rock.
our shadows unspool across the cavern wall.
they're flickering, shifting. they won't hold still.

(interlude: the swan describes an invasive species)

several methods are used to cull an unwanted swan population. shotguns, primarily, for the ease of it, for the fun of it, the harsh joy of sighting down the barrel and taking us where we float, our necks arced to our mates, our kingdom of weeds below us. kinder cullers addle our eggs, dipping them whole into corn oil to smother the porous shells, robbing the embryos of oxygen, failing them in gentle smother. still others set dogs on our young, kick over our nests, poison us with tainted feed. america killed her trumpeter swans, but she doesn't love us, her mute replacements: so beautiful, so hungry, so vehement in defending ourselves. helen, i see you. hatched from an egg, paddling ever since. born in a land that doubts your claim to it.

helen of troy goes parking with the defensive tackle

first time he asked, i got in the car—pontiac minotaur,
eight vees under a hood long enough to nest at least
four swans, two up and two back, or one single swan
beating her wings. i was all swans in those days,
all slump next to mom on the park bench, all yeah yeah
sure okay whatever, breadcrumbs lobbed wristwise
to the pond mob, militia of orange beaks. a full-grown swan
can drop a body fast as headlights. a full-grown swan
knows where to land on a friday night, knows
how to cheer, and for whom, and what to do when
her halfback brother heaves his pads off the tailgate
and says *i warned him to quit looking at you*. but fifteen
is the age for looking back. oh, this was way before
the big cheese—high school roll of bleacher feet,
friday battles we waterloo'd with dismal dependability.
the depths of that weekly loss, like white feathers
on the tongue. the rage of it. when i got in the car,
i thought he'd been crying. i thought: robert redford,
andy gibb, that monkey they strapped down and launched
into space, what was his name, turkey or ham, some kind
of lunchmeat, something with the salt to ram a car
into drive. eighty-five out of town, wet sneer of engine,
gearshift squeezed up and up. i watched our old familiar hills
open their mouths and swallow the moon,
and when it struggled free again there always came
a new set of teeth. a full-grown swan has few natural
predators. dogs, mostly. raccoons, which seems unlikely,
given how much they joke with their friends, how they
hold open doors and almost win football games. and if
he didn't stop? who would know, who would come
to chase me down? he parked in the wreck

of just-razed tobacco, unbuckled his seat belt, took my
jaw in his grip. i can't remember what i wanted.
homecoming, maybe. prom. or maybe it was the black fields,
velvet smother, how the night crept inside anything
with wings. his fingers in my hair, bright pulse of pain.
i thought: i don't—
but what did i know? maybe i did.
the end was so quick. blinding headlights in the rearview,
tires in the dry dirt. my door yanked open. *get out*,
my brother said, jersey still drenched, his face
an iron bar, and i was so glad, and so furious.

helen of troy runs to piggly wiggly

oh, we're always out of something, cheerios or bananas, orange tang,
dunkaroos for the lunchbox. the pig is the place where all desire
is consummated, each want made fat, made starch, made bone-in-flesh,
shrink-wrapped and sold at four ninety-nine, checkbook balanced
right at the till. beloved land of madonna on the speakers. country
of women with cursive lists. everyone i've ever known nurses
their children from these shelves, pushing loads of accreting weight.
everyone i've yet to meet. i high-step through the aisles,
nursemaid to bread loaves, coupons purse-holstered and waiting.
sing, muse, of the manager's special, two-for-one on yogurt cups,
little debbies leaping for the cart. at the oranges, our hands meet.
i keep my eyes on the bin, embarrassment of juices,
the way his hands move over slick skin. our kingdom is divided
into pride and shame, cash and stamps, home and away, all the girls
and helen herself, you remember helen, prom queen helen,
feathered helen, grown up strange. the linoleum shines so bright
i can see my foot take each step, the bottom of the shoe descend
to its reflection until the soles kiss and merge, their dark lengths
pressed together without a molecule of air between them.
each box i choose, i pay for. each apple i take
is from the top of the stack, lifted away so quick the others tremble
but hold their shape, forgetting they were once more than they are.

about the affair again

i.

he said have you ever been north before

                            and i hadn't.

ii.

winter sewed me into her lungs.

i felt each gust,
each gasp.

iii.

my husband, he'll bomb squad. he'll sniffer dog.
he'll fly in the army. he'll call up the fuzz.
he'll swat team, he'll fire truck, he'll ambulance.
i'll wake up one morning to green berets.

but he doesn't.

iv.

i'll tell you what it was.   it was a blank space.

                                it was the shape of that blank space.

                                                  its ridges and valleys.

(interlude: the swan describes the war)

the first day, the big cheese sends half a can of waspkill into the nest on the porch. not truly a nest. a clump of gold and black bodies moving over and around each other, fixed at the join of siding and gutter. they fall to the cement with a sound like *pap, pap, pap,* stiff brown wings locked back against their abdomens. but there is a new clump on the swing chain the second day, and he has to buy more cans of waspkill from home depot. this nest rises when he begins to spray. he stands in the drive and shoots them out of the air with quick streams from the can, like hunting doves in the season, and he takes them all, or most of them, enough of them that his hands are burning where the can is leaking at the nozzle. but on the third day there are more. they have come from somewhere else, or maybe they are the same hornets, knocked down but not killed, stubbornly mounding up on the porch light. on this day the kid has to go to school. he takes her around back and makes her run past the porch, run to the bus. *don't stop*, he roars, when she cranes her neck to look at the seething mass of them. *faster. get out of here.* he goes back to home depot. on the fourth day he walks the perimeter like a warden, spray locked in his peeling fist. he doesn't see anything, but he wets down the roofline anyway, spraying in one continuous stream. he peers under eaves and behind peels of paint. he looks inside the gutter. when he finds the hornets, there are only three or four left. they aren't moving. they are huddled together where the roof curls over the front walk. he sprays them, but they don't fall. he keeps spraying. the white foam builds up around the hornets until he can't see their bodies anymore. where is helen? i don't know, or else i would tell you. i would be telling you about helen and not about the big cheese. but i don't know where she has gone.

one more thing about the affair

a golden shovel from *Iliad* 3.199, tr. Robert Fagles

he has a house on some land. i

walk in the morning with his dog,   bare spits of rock where my shoes don't

hold their grip,   acres burned by dumping from the cement plant,   chemical blame

churned into the soil.   i think you

will be happy here, he told me, fist hauling back on the dog's collar.   the dog and i

roam wide, belly of winter-black trees that hold

the wrecks of half-sunk stills, skeletal deer, the

bone-clean breath of gods

of starving.   i can't hear any voices. i can't find a way to

call up my own blame.

the spartan women discuss the stranger

flickering, shifting, then holding itself still
when the birds grow wary, a coyote
troubles the edges of the drainage pond.
we loose the farm dogs to savage its heels
and shrug to each other at the feed store—
animals obey their instincts. geese and swans,
for instance, are perfect parents, mating
for life until something sunk-ribbed and
starving breaks their vows. the day she left,
we examined the thing from every angle,
this puzzle of biology: abnormal,
shocking, a swan who'd do the stalking,
a coyote, strange to these parts, willing
to be stolen from his life, taken away.

helen of troy returns to sparta

Musée National Gustave Moreau: Study of Helen, *Gustave Moreau*

in the final mile i made the cab pull over
to get out and walk. i didn't know if a body
could survive such a walk. that was the charm
of the experiment, that i might die from it
and thus render myself the answer
to some great mystery. maybe you have also
felt it building inside you: a red pressure
within the channels of flesh, a kind of biting
heat, this conviction of your own
consequence. crows gathered
for our twilight processional. here was
the mcdonald's, the wendy's, the mural
with black horses. here was the turnoff
where the kid had her school.
the chain-link park fence.
the dandelions threading through tins
of chaw. above me clouds pressed
into each other's arms and held the rain
on their shoulders, and the wind when it came
scraped away shreds of myself
but at the same time delivered old shreds
back to me, old stretches of skin that fit
themselves to the holes i'd been guarding,
like jam settling into a canning jar.
i turned onto our street. maybe you are also
a person who longs for diagnosis.
i thought about our sputtering porch light,
how it would blind me, how it would shine
through my body in burning spears.

helen of troy joins the ice fishing trip

he won't leave me alone
anymore. therefore the boots,
therefore the coat, the shack
penning two. his hands
on the saw, layers of cold
lifted up and away. his touch
on the lantern-key.
swimming darkness,
lake's creaking groan.
you know how to bait
your own hook, he says.
blade pushed through
wet softness. i watch him
bring up the first body.
how it thrashes, how it
leaps in the air.

one last thought on the affair

the light was

        the same.   and the half-light.

helen of troy's turn to judge

much later, when the clothes were washed and dried,
three women came in their nakedness so i could choose
from among them the most beautiful. i should say

the cat had just pissed on the carpet, our old cat,
a fighting tom come in from the wars, and so when
the women found me i was hunched on my knees

pressing paper towels into the shag, the bright crack
of ammonia through the air like a train whistle.
i wasn't afraid. the women no longer looked like me,

so i no longer longed to hurt them for it. i should say
that by then the world was already dead, my brothers
and cousins, the boys i knew at school: a great cloud

that lowered itself across the tobacco, threw its shanks
against the window glass, opened the earth
in short dark rips. it's best to put pressure where

the pool is deepest, push your hand down firmly
while the gold siphons away, a warm dripping pad
you can bag and disappear. the women were holding

small white boxes, and the lid of each box spelled out
what was inside in a language without subtlety or art.
knowledge. power. sex, this last picked out in rubies

and sapphires, a script that shimmered with a strange
inner heat, baking the room, unmaking it. the cat leapt
to the kitchen table to bat the surface with unsheathed

claws. if there is a mystery to which box was chosen,
i apologize. i should have said more. i should have said
that music rose from the third box in sweeping arias,

that the smell of sea air and thunderstorms rolled
from beneath the lid. i should have said that i knew
the box because it was mine, given to me as a young girl

and kept safe beneath my bed ever since. i was angry.
i wanted her bleeding, the woman who had stolen from me,
who wore a face that was familiar the way a mountain

is familiar, loved so long it softens into background blur.
i yanked the box from her hands, but she wouldn't let go.
we held it together, she and i, our fingers stroking

beneath the base. she seemed glad to share the load.
it was a heavy box; i'd forgotten the heft of it, the way
it dragged at the lower spine, like a tumor or a baby.

i wondered if she'd ever looked inside. the woman, was she
beautiful? it hardly mattered. she'd already turned away,
studying the view with a jeweler's eye: the empty yard,

the empty drive, the cat-killed sparrow dragged to the stoop.

(interlude: the swan describes the ouroboros)

the serpent is cool to the touch, heavy in the hand, her muscular body rippling like wind through the hillside's damp underbelly. the preacher lifts the serpent from the gunnysack into the air. this is a moment of great danger: the preacher is safe so long as belief transfigures the believer, arming him with a palm the serpent will not strike; so long as belief rewrites the serpent, erasing fear, rage, the darkening need for retribution. the serpent twists and stretches, doubles back. the serpent hangs in the void. i'm looking out from your eyes, helen, but the landscape keeps changing. i see a house, i see a palace. i see chevrolets and long ships, streetlights and torches. there are fields wherever i look, watered and fed on monsanto or blood. when the preacher opens his mouth, the sermon is delivered in many different tongues, riding the static of the serpent's rattling tail. echoes shiver and dissolve. the congregation is very far away, and at the same time so close it is inside him, it is filling up the vessels of his body with infinite sound and infinite hurt. the preacher returns the serpent to the sack. now is a moment of greater danger still: he has held his fate inside his hands, and now his hands are empty. they open and close uselessly in the chill air, red and plush, unbitten.

helen of troy catches reruns

day gone, work gone, dinner gone—
we spent our evenings on the couch
with the tv guide and the lights turned low,
cheers, golden girls, all in the family,
people whose lives recycled trouble
in thirty-minute increments, a fresh disaster
twice an hour, some great generational curse
working itself out through the medium
of their bodies. *have mercy*, jesse said,
and then he kissed a girl so perfectly
that full house had to cut to commercial.
the kid was in bed. the dishes were dripping
in their rack. the curtains were open,
our house a backlit diorama for the education
of thieves and dog walkers, a stage set
for a play with no intermission. onscreen,
cindy crawford sold us pepsi at a gas station,
her eyes like smears of black charcoal,
her throat working at the center of the camera's
hungry eye. my husband hissed out a breath.
the line of skin above his collar flickered
in the television glow; i put my mouth to it.
i wanted to do this, a fact that seemed obvious
to me at the time, although years later
i would replay the episode in my head,
turning the plot inside out, trying
to understand the setup, the punchline.

helen of troy recalls the tenth date

probably it was dinner and dancing
or dinner and music or dinner and
i don't know, some other postscript
to the initial round of consumption,
shooting or drinks or riding around
in his truck while he pointed out
land the company was buying up.
that's not important. what i want to
remember is yanking the chain off
the door to get to him on the stoop,
evening sun slicing through every
chink in the slow-rotting pergola
overhead, den of carpenter bees
and termites eating their lives
straight into the bone. he smiled
at me, wire frames and pinstripes
and the same kind of watch my
father wore, and when he put out
his hand and said *let's get the hell
out of here*, i grabbed on so tight
he cussed and had to shake me off
his fingers. it wasn't always so
gory, is what i'm saying. or maybe
i mean that if there were problems,
i was still digging their roots.

helen of troy honeymoons on st. john

each hour broken around a rooster's crow. bloody arm
of poinciana framed in the window, red petals across our salt-stiff
towels, small wasp of sand between fingernail and quick, throbbing faintly,
worked in deep. the cloud cover does not abate once. blue throws itself upward
to a building storm, rubs its belly against the white sheet,
tongue rasping up foam. i see how the shore contracts,
softens, allows. is this your first time, he asks me,
and i almost say no, think of your truck, think two three four times
of our turnoff in the woods, waffle house sign rearing gold goddess lightning
beyond the next bend, but instead i say yes, yes, oh
lover, be careful with me. yes is the answer to every
question. the sea through the taxicab windshield.
the rain that throws itself down all at once. the warblers
in the hibiscus, the serpentine switchbacks,
the woman at the desk handing us flowers, shall i leave you
for the morning, shall i touch you soon, touch you now, pile your lap
with bone-bleach coral, battered and dead, washed up on the tide?
there are still donkeys on this island. they climb the steepest roads
in family trains, line of gray yoked to a skipper,
sure of each palm and calabash, many footfalls sending up dust.
waking alone, i flail out my arms,
grabbing about me for anything to hold, anyone who may be near.

the spartan women discuss the kid

if she's stolen from her life, taken away,
installed with the aunt, maybe, fed on
humility three meals a day, hair cut,
new clothes, name whittled down to a one-
syllable noise, she'll haunt us so gently
we'll forget she can levitate. it's all
survivable after the first shock. you start
bubble-wrapping your belly-meat,
oiling the hinges to dampen the shriek.
poor unmothered somebody, transparent
below the jugular—bless that child,
then chop her for parts. at one time, truly,
we ourselves were girls. that was many
years ago, and we have since recovered.

helen of troy reigns over chuck e. cheese

the kid's too old, for one thing—rodent mafia more the purview
of tinies in smock dresses still built small enough to wedge
their arms up the claw machine when the damn thing cheats
them out of a chuck-branded wiffle ball or some such similar
landfill pre-designee—and for another the thought of doing
ol' mom a nice turn must turn the tum something fierce
judging strictly by the explosion of gut-deep soul sighs issuing
from the back seat like she's huffing black death from the depths
of her small intestine, but she's here, isn't she, she came, didn't she,
which is more filial piety than i presumed from any kind of preteen
prima donna, much less one with a mama like i turned out to be,
so it's less of a surprise and more of a darwinian inevitability
when she vanishes the millisecond we're parked and unbuckled
and shuttled through the swing doors yawning open like the hinges
on one of those medieval lemon juicers they fed on witches
and sinners, just haring off into the aural overload of clink-clang-
ka-ching echoing from every inch of the jumped-up kiddie casino
we're meant to be colonizing to fête little kenneth carmichael
on his seventh birthday as if i don't know exactly what missus
down-the-street meant by mailing me that four-by-four
of cardstock with date and time and *rsvps please!!* above a photo
of her own whey-faced offspring cheshire-catting in a technicolor
orgy of kinko's profligacy, but i'm no chicken-liver i'm no
yellow-belly i sally forth *without* the social buffer of my fugitive
daughter straight into the cursèd heart of hell's own watering hole
while behind me and before me and all around me springs forth
a veritable symphony of whispering, every mother of every
sugar-happy small fry south of the kentucky border firing off
like a baking soda volcano to see yours truly pirouetting among
the salt of the earth like proverbs 31 and not a devil-licking jezebel
bound straight for the fiery pits i mean how dare i show my face

how dare i leave my house how dare i steer my greedy two-timing sin-
skin through a room where innocent children are picking their noses,
exactly the sort of local commotion i expected from all and sundry
except for the small but crucial detail that in my head i'd pictured
myself gliding among the jealous ranks of no-account pond ducks
like a noble swan bedecked in white while now cometh the hour
i'm feeling more along the lines of a broken-legged field mouse
marked for death by the circling hawks, and i don't blame the kid
for going ghost—i'm sure i'd've done the same were i the scion
of the town slut arrived home from weeks of unauthorized
pornographic ignominy, crawling back to her slighted husband
like a flighty bit of chaff of which the worthy wheat
had most certainly been well-rid—but man-eater or no, in the jaws
of the maternal sanctum of first-baptist-ladies'-association busybodies
i suddenly need my daughter like i need my own skin, like seeing
her scowling face is going to be the only thing that keeps all my
wobbly insides from spilling across the sprite-sticky linoleum
like the bottom ripping out of a garbage bag, and i think i last
about ninety seconds quivering at the center of the holy maelstrom
of gleeful gossip before turning tail to hunt her down, this girl
who might or might not hate every cell in my she-viper body
but is—i'm absolutely sure—worth more in one unhappy scowl
than a whole chuck e.'s worth of pristine southern church ladies,
and although i'm sure it's no secret that i can be somewhat of an
indifferent mother, i really do think if i find her now i'll tell her
everything, i'll tell her the ugliest and most beautiful parts
of walking out that door and coming home again,
i'll spill my guts after all right here in the middle of a rat-themed
las vegas and won't care one bald tail for the pearl-clutching
conniptions of any number of other women who weren't raised
in my home in my clothes looking back at my face in my mirror,
who don't know me at all, but of course when i finally clock the kid
burrowed away at the very top of the foam-padded play tower

i don't say any of those things whatsoever, i just hoist my too-adult
mother-self up the climbing ropes to join her in her crow's nest,
and when i've folded up real small right next to her and touched
my fingers to the fraying hem of her tina turner t-shirt, she gives
me this little squiggle of mouth movement that's not exactly
a smile but sort of could be in the right light, and we look down
together over a pizza-scented kingdom of grease-streaked children
and their harried minders who from all the way up here seem like
nothing more than flecks of glittered light thrown by the disco ball
spinning above the wide wooden stage, where to frenzied cheering
the animatronics are taking up their instruments and beginning to play.

helen of troy makes peace with the kudzu

my father foxholed me in the lee of the porch,
gloved and hungry, ready for battle,
straining at the leash until he launched me
into the yearly war. i sprang at them,
the tendrils threatening the house,
the little questing outriders opening
their mouths to eat. i yanked them.
i hurt them. i beat them back,
arms streaked with dirt, following their line
to the great press of the mother vine,
the carpet of vegetation toppling our fences,
creeping along in inches, in yards.
the blanket of it. the smother. i tell you
i was raised among all breeds of weapon—
hand trowels and knife-blade shovels,
weedeaters, hedge trimmers, chemicals
in ranks of deadliness, their attendant
nozzles and hoses, and so when i tell you
i became myself a single sharp edge,
perhaps you'll hold in your mind the crèche
that honed me. an animal hunger.
a green grasp with shadow beneath,
a moving thing fed on new gulps of land.
i walked out into the mass of it, boots
to my knees against the coiled mines
of copperheads, my mother behind me,
watching the sky for a white spread
of wings. i grew my whole life in a house
death longed to touch with one soft finger,
and when i looked out at the building wave,
i thought, *do it.* the world around me

hunkered under the wrong spread of life,
and yet i saw that it was living,
edges softened, blanks filled in—a sphere
that begged my absence, that collected
my childhood in its outstretched hands
and pushed it under the skin of itself,
hidden and repurposed, folded away,
breathing gently under combs of wind.

the end of the affair

Musée National Gustave Moreau: Helen at the Scaean Gate, *Gustave Moreau*

on the night i knew was our last, we sat down to a feast
in the smoking section of the perkins beside the city walls,
which differed from the perkins in my town only in the number
of dead men who ate there. the air-con was running pretty good,
stiffing up the hair on my shins and souping the windows
thick enough to hide what the sky was doing outside,
a mean mess of clouds tinting themselves yellow and gray
and yellow again, galloping above a world pre-flinched
for its next bruising. he lit a cigarette and passed it to me,
which was a new thing i was doing, another small light
flashing frenetically in the background. i was so hungry
in my body. i wanted more than the glut on the laminated menu,
identical in every offering to the one at the perkins back home,
the same meals exhumed from a walk-in's dark freeze.
columns of smoke rose from every table. the booth heaved
with plates of grease and blood. when the hail began
at last to hurl itself downward, it struck against
the wood paneling with a hollow call i felt in my belly,
a pounding that signaled the end of what we were eating,
whatever it was we were putting in our mouths.

helen of troy explains to the gods

gods of old worlds, gods of our worlds: i try to tell you
important things, things that happened, hours emerging
with claws and fangs. i've been talking to you all along,
i think, packing my thoughts with ice and fluid

like a series of hearts en route to their new chests.
when i say "i," i'm describing an animal who eats
when she is fed. an alarm that sounds for anyone
who's listening. gods of empty pews, if you're listening,

i should tell you i belong to a shrinking town, every day
a girl gone, pickup lost over hills that cut their shapes
from the sky in floods of deeper darkness. a get-out town.
a valley you leave as soon as you're grown.

gods of difficult things, i'm out there still, foraging
in the threads of the world for a story i like better
than the one i've been telling. i'm working in the trenches
of my own future, stitching together pieces of bone

and oracle to run down the threat of what might
happen next. of what i might do. gods of ugly things.
gods of what is still growing within. i am speaking
these words from inside a prayer, a scraped-out cavity

ready for filling. why are we even going to church,
says the big cheese. why are we alive at all, says the kid.
she says the things he says, these days. she fights me
on her church clothes, tights and frilly socks, skirts i iron

with desperate calm. she wants to wear stirrup pants
and jellies. she wants to listen to music all day
or practice ballet in her room. i brush her hair
while she tells me she hates me. i fix a butterfly clip

in her braid, tiny springs keeping its wings shivering
in the nest of sunlight around her crown. even a breath
will make them dance. gods of hands that hold other hands,
i had her young. i was twenty-one, and she was a thing

i did not understand. my life was a thing i did not
understand. i was married. i was happy. i was so happy
i was burning alive from the inside, looking for a way
to carve my life apart so i wouldn't have to live it anymore.

gods of the greyhound bus and all its riders,
there's a road into town and a road out of town,
although you can come and go by the same road,
or by opposite roads, or in fact by no road at all if you leave

your car by the stoplight and go on foot into the dark
and wild places where no one has cleared brush
for a baskin-robbins or a walgreens. actually there are
ten roads into town and ten roads leaving. actually

there are state routes and highways, mack trucks
that bull through the wet air on their way from somewhere
to somewhere, but they don't stop, or if they do, it's only
for gas at the pilot with the mcdonald's next door,

brought to a halt for a moment in the fading light,
huge metal bodies perfectly quiet, hot to the touch,

trembling lightly with the weight of what's inside.
gods of running. gods of coming home. i was one

of the stream of girls melting back into our old lives,
rib-kicked by the world we wanted so badly to hold
in our hands, nothing big, nothing lavish, nothing more
than our due: one single calendar page of sunshine

and bright sand, booze-dark sea stretching out into a song
we can't sing but have been humming all our lives.
i try to tell you important things. i try to tell you when i feel
myself slipping. last week the kid's teacher asked whether

there might be any trouble at home. this was after the kid
reared back and fired her elbow into a girl's jaw
at the end of homeroom, bone against bone, shrieking
and snarling and tussling on the ground. gods of birds

who speak in human voices, i do not want to watch
her walk through a life of small mercies and small choices.
i want each tooth spit up clean and delivered to her palm
to plant as she chooses, or not to plant, or to swallow

off her tongue like a cold and far-off star. i dream
and i don't stop dreaming. night crushes down on our house
like a boot on a lit cigarette, and yet when the heel lifts away
the embers are still glowing. who

                                        am i? i am asking
for the sake of research. i'd like to take down all opinions,
everything they might whisper in my ear when they think
the teacher isn't looking. who am i

                              becoming? gods of suns
still climbing to their zenith, i'm trying to explain myself to you.
i caught tadpoles as a little child. i kept them in a bucket
beside the wide lake. i watched as they grew legs

and flung themselves over the edge, freedom a thing
that first required a great fall. gods of this church.
gods of all the others. i am falling and i am asking
for so much: a hymn. a pardon. a soft place to land.

the spartan women discuss helen of troy

years ago—though she afterward recovered—
a girl was born who was not a swan.
thick-boned, earth-bound, she looked every minute
over her shoulder for the real life
she was promised, but her neck was too short
and she could not see it.   ah, helen.
when you're dead we'll cherish you again.
we'll touch your face in our photo albums
and tell each other what you did, how you
climbed the tallest hill and sprang from the summit,
a shining smear of predestination,
wingless, featherless, taunting your own fall.
we'll remember how you launched yourself:
beautiful and suffering. mortal as a wound.

helen of troy plants near the mailbox

a golden shovel from *Iliad* 6.424–426, tr. Robert Fagles

i needed something that thrived on neglect. i needed god
to send me the kind of life that would survive my mothering, planted
deeper than i could reach, a
cradle dug beyond the killing
lance of my own attention. it's hard to say what doom
will take. it's hard to prune the rot within
yourself, sucker leaf, aphid grub, a drain that moves from me to us,
a kind of withering both
fragile and all-consuming, a sucking away from the inside. i am so
sorry, i told the nursery. i am a destroyer of even
the hardiest of vines. and yet, and yet. i'm here for
bulbs and bare roots, generations
of seeds from the bones of our hills, earth-fed promises still
calling down the line, unborn
seasons nested one within the other. in my house, we
need more than morning sun. we need green things with a will
to live,
dirt-bound fighters dragging themselves to the light, blooming in
ragged fistfuls, mouths held wide in ribbons of song.

god

planted

a

killing

doom

within

us

both,

so

even

for

generations

still

unborn,

we

will

live

in

song.

Afterword

Because I grew up a quiet, book-eating girl with unrestricted access to several branches of Memphis Public Libraries, I was well-versed in Greek and Roman myth long before ninth-grade English with Mrs. Bell. That was the year of Edith Hamilton and Robert Fagles, a whole class of fourteen-year-old girls punching through both the *Iliad* and the *Odyssey* in about six weeks. I already knew my gods and monsters, my heroes, my lineages. I'd been dutifully translating my way through the Cambridge Latin Course textbooks since seventh grade. I thought I was ready. But how could I have been? I was young, raw, and anchorless: easy prey for a carnivorous story looking for its next meal, and the Trojan War has a bottomless appetite. I fell into its mouth that breakneck year, and it's been carrying me around ever since.

The Trojan War is the sticky center of a spiderweb so large its edges reach back into the beginnings of Greek myth and forward into the rise and reign of Rome. The gist of the story is this: The Trojan prince Paris awards the goddess of love Aphrodite top prize in a beauty contest among her peers, and as payment for this favor, she promises him the most beautiful woman in the world as his wife—Helen, a half-mortal child of Zeus. The problem being, of course, that Helen is already married to Menelaus, the Greek king of Sparta. Paris arrives in Sparta as a guest and abducts Helen (or perhaps they run away together—accounts vary), and Menelaus rallies the other kings and heroes of Greece to sail for Troy and take her back. The result is a ten-year war surrounding the walled city, "hurling down to the House of Death so many sturdy souls, / great fighters' souls . . . their bodies carrion, / feasts for the dogs and birds,"[1] an avalanche of butchery that ends with the annihilation of Troy. It's a story about honor and fate, about how easy it is to kill and die. Ancient Greek and Roman audiences were steeped in Troy's tangle of legends, and even modern readers generally understand the basic plot. This familiarity makes the story one of the world's perfect tragedies: We enter the war with our hearts already broken for Greeks and Trojans alike,

---

[1] *Iliad* 1.3–5, tr. Robert Fagles

knowing that Patroclus will die, Hector will die, Achilles will die, little baby Astyanax will die. Knowing that all the women of Troy will soon be dragged down to the beach to join Briseïs and the other captured war prizes: raped, enslaved, divvied up among the victors. Well, all the women except Helen.

No, not Helen. She walks out of the ruins of Troy and returns to the throne of Sparta beside her former husband, Menelaus. The women who surround her—elderly Hecuba, prophetic Cassandra, the perfect princess Andromache—all suffer unimaginable fates, ending their stories slain or enslaved. But Helen simply goes home, as if the past decade were just a bad dream. Maddening Helen! Helen for whom the war was started. Helen in whose name a generation of men fought and died. Euripides's tragic play *The Trojan Women* is one long wail of grief, wherein Hecuba tries in vain to convince Menelaus to enact justice upon Helen for all her sins: for leaving her first husband, for refusing to leave her second even while Hecuba's many sons perished in payment, for her "opulent appetites" that make her "hell for cities, burning hell for homes."[2] In the eyes of Troy and Greece alike, Helen *is* the war, the embodiment of their suffering. Legend says Menelaus very nearly did choose vengeance, chasing Helen through Troy with a drawn sword. But one glimpse of her otherworldly beauty at the crucial moment stopped his blade, and there was nothing left to do but to bring his slippery bride back across the sea.

I've always struggled with Helen, even while studying classics back in college. I often think about the 1888 painting *Helen at the Scaean Gate* by the French symbolist Gustave Moreau, in which a Helen of monstrous size stands before the smoking walls of Troy. At her feet lie crushed and spattered the bloody remains of those caught up in her wake: death-dealing Helen, the demigod daughter of Zeus, never truly brought to account. But is this the best interpretation of Helen's role in the war? After all, did Helen leave Sparta willingly, absconding in the night with her lover, cheering on the Trojans as they beat back the Greeks come to drag her home? Or was she abducted by Paris and kept prisoner behind the walls for ten long years while

[2] *The Trojan Women*, Euripides, tr. Alan Shapiro

she wept for her former life? Or should we best understand Helen as nothing more than the pawn of Aphrodite, a doll handed to Paris as payment for a victory in a contest among Olympians? Or is Helen something else entirely, a mercurial, half-human entity loyal only to herself, the freest agent in the entire Trojan War because she is the only one not bound by honor? Helen is complicated. She defies easy answers and easy scholarship. The doomed women around her are certainly much more sympathetic figures, and it can be tempting to leave Helen well enough alone.

I myself certainly left her alone. Back in 2020, as the world ended, I was once again living inside the *Iliad*. The world was also ending inside the *Iliad*, of course, so the plains and beaches were less of a departure from and more of a simple transmutation of my own community's circumstances. I sat out on my porch with Rocky the dog in the hours between increasingly dire Zoom calls, breathing in the dense Southern humidity of Coastal Georgia and writing persona poems in the voices of women from the Trojan War. It was a vaguely therapeutic project, allowing the pandemic pressure valve to release through old agonies from Bronze Age Greece, hurts that belonged to Andromache, Cassandra, Helen's sister Clytemnestra, and Clytemnestra's poor daughter Iphigenia, who was sacrificed to the goddess Artemis by her father for wind to launch the fleet of ships toward Troy. Helen's name lurked beneath the whole endeavor, untouched. I wasn't sure what to do with her. I wasn't sure I *wanted* to do anything with her. For a full year, I ignored her while I published or shelved the other poems from the project and started on new work with different themes. I changed jobs, moved home to Tennessee, bought a house. And in the summer of 2021, in a kind of manic daze, I suddenly dove for my notebook and wrote seven Helen poems in a row.

But the voice that emerged had nothing to do with Bronze Age Greece. It was too familiar for that, too much like a woman I might have run into one day at the grocery store or the bank. The sun began to rise over a landscape I recognized, illuminating the world of my childhood in 1990s Tennessee: station wagons and backyard barbecues and Friday-night football and neighbors who look at you sideways in church. This stifled, hilarious, cliff-edge housewife marched onto the page and introduced herself as Helen of Troy.

She brought the whole gang with her, the full cast of my beloved mythos, to walk around a town that had certainly never seen their like. Helen had a story to tell, and all I had to do was keep writing until she'd said her piece. I hadn't wanted much to do with Helen; now I couldn't look away. The Helen of myth might always be a question mark, but this Tennessee girl was an exclamation point. She was an imperfect mother and wife, an imperfect woman grasping for agency in imperfect ways, tangled inextricably in the plot threads of the Trojan War. Mythology hands Helen's agency to Aphrodite, who gives her away, to Paris, who steals her away, and to Menelaus, who scoops her away from the wreckage of Troy and sails her back to her former throne. In 1993, though, her story was old, but her decisions were new—and were, inarguably, her own.

In the Sparta of myth, Helen's departure set off a long and grinding war, shipfuls of men launched across the water to snatch back a woman of stained reputation. Before Helen's father gave her in marriage to one among the host of lords competing for her hand, he took Odysseus's advice to require that every man swear an oath to fight for the chosen husband if someone ever stole Helen away. No sooner had Paris spirited Helen out of Sparta than Menelaus cashed in on that promise, forcing every former suitor to raise their levies for war. But there is no war brewing in Sparta, Tennessee, no "vast armada gathered, moored at Aulis, / freighted with slaughter bound for Priam's Troy."[3] Instead, this Tennessee town holds nothing more than an abandoned, powerless husband with no oath to call in, no army to revenge his humiliation. All he has is his injured pride, a wound that sickens, turns inward, curdles him into frustrated inaction. It is winter for Menelaus when Helen leaves—and winter, too, for Helen, having left.

For Helen, this deep freeze begins in Sparta and does not break, to her surprise, past the borders of her former life. How to understand Helen of Troy in 1993, choosing to go, and once gone, choosing to come home? Is she happy? Or is she just as miserable as she was before the affair? Does she even quite know the answer herself? Is happiness, in the end, even a useful

---

[3] *Iliad* 2.356–357, tr. Robert Fagles

metric with which to measure Helen's life? Our Helen is still unique, set apart, special—but not special enough to watch the tide of history turn on the axis of her body. Instead, she must turn herself, and allow history to fall around her like snow.

The legend of the Trojan War has been told and retold for more than three thousand years. Permutations, additions, side stories, and revisionist histories abound in every era. Statius, Ovid, and Virgil added their contributions; so did Chaucer and Berlioz and *Xena: Warrior Princess*. Even in the ancient world, a counterlegend sprang up asserting that Helen never went to Troy at all. Instead, she waited out the war blamelessly in Egypt while a ghostly clone, an *eidolon*, went to Troy in her place (this "ghost-helen" makes an appearance in "and another thing about the affair"). The events and personalities of the Trojan War are not matters of historical record we can track in the same way we can, for example, Churchill on the eve of World War II. Nevertheless, historians generally agree that Troy was a city in modern-day Hisarlik, Türkiye, destroyed many times through the ages, and that whichever of its destructions corresponded with the Trojan War of legend likely had little to do with a tussle over the most beautiful woman in the world. In the absence of facts, all we have are stories, each a new thread woven into a tapestry that was not finished with the fall of Troy or the fall of Rome, that isn't complete today and won't be tomorrow, either. All of us who sharpen our pencils and turn again to the page with these characters are writing into that long tradition. We're raising eidolons, real and not-real, tales that move and breathe and stand side by side, speaking Troy into the future.

Acknowledgments

My deep gratitude to the journals and editors who have published poems from this book, occasionally in earlier forms or under different titles.

Alaska Quarterly Review—helen of troy returns to sparta

The Arkansas International—helen of troy is asked to the spring formal

The Atlantic—helen of troy meets the big cheese

Bat City Review—one more thing about the affair

Booth—helen of troy makes an entrance

Cave Wall—and another thing about the affair

The Commuter (Electric Literature)—helen of troy feuds with the neighborhood *and* helen of troy makes peace with the kudzu

Cream City Review—about the affair again

HAD—helen of troy runs the station wagon into a ditch

Hunger Mountain—helen of troy's new whirlpool washing machine *and* helen of troy watches jurassic park in theaters

The Kenyon Review—helen of troy goes ice fishing, helen of troy calls her sister, another thing about the affair, helen of troy in february, *and* helen of troy avoids her school reunion

LitMag—about the affair, the end of the affair, *and* helen of troy explains to the gods

The Missouri Review—helen of troy catalogues her pregnancy cravings

Narrative—helen of troy's turn to judge *and* helen of troy runs to piggly wiggly

New Letters—helen of troy gets the news from her sister, helen of troy cleans up after the barbecue, *and* helen of troy reigns over chuck e. cheese

New Ohio Review—helen of troy recalls the tenth date

Poetry Daily—helen of troy calls her sister *(reprint)*

Poetry Northwest—helen of troy in the delivery ward

Puerto del Sol—helen of troy surfs the net *and* helen of troy plants near the mailbox

Redivider—(interlude: the swan describes the war)

The Sewanee Review—helen of troy folds laundry in a dim room *and* helen of troy cranks the volume on "like a prayer" in the ballet studio parking lot

Smartish Pace—(interlude: the swan describes an invasive species)

The Southampton Review—(interlude: the swan describes the harvest) *and* (interlude: the swan describes the ouroboros)

Tahoma Literary Review—helen of troy recovers at st. francis

Washington Square Review—helen of troy goes parking with the defensive tackle

ZYZZYVA—helen of troy tells her mother it's a graduation girls' trip and drives alone to the clinic in nashville *and* helen of troy catches reruns

To my family, for believing: Rocky, Barbara, Will, Tommy, Patricia, John.

To the friends who read and championed these poems: Angie, Neha, Kayla, Claire, Emily.

To Kelsey Day, my friend-agent-friend who made this dream possible, and the Aragi family.

To Emily Polson, the editor who saw into the heart of this book.

To the Scribner team, who printed my heart in paper and ink.

To Helen, who has millennia left to live.

Notes

The setting of *Helen of Troy, 1993*, is entirely fictional. The Sparta, Tennessee, of the poems is not a representation of the real-world Sparta of White County, Tennessee, a beautiful spot on the Calfkiller River.

Where lines from Homer's *Iliad* have been quoted or used in golden shovels, I have pulled from the 1998 Penguin Books edition of Robert Fagles's 1990 translation, the same beat-up old copy I've been dragging around since the ninth grade. In the golden shovel "helen of troy plants near the mailbox," where Fagles uses the word *Zeus*, I have substituted the word *God*.

Helen and her brother Pollux were conceived after Zeus raped their mother, Leda, while in the form of a swan. In the myth tradition, therefore, the swan is a menacing symbol of erotic danger. In this book, I have reclaimed and repurposed the image of the swan.

"helen of troy makes an entrance" retells the myth of Helen's birth. She and her siblings were said to have hatched from eggs, and shrines around the ancient world dedicated to Helen or her siblings sometimes featured relics of their eggshells.

When read together, the poem series "the spartan women discuss" forms a sonnet crown. The first poem in the series, "the spartan women discuss the local waterfowl," is based on the myth that a swan is silent her whole life until she's dying, at which point she sings the most beautiful song ever heard.

When the time came for Helen to marry, her father held a competition for all the most eligible bachelors in Greece, who arrived in Sparta with piles of treasure and ready to compete for her hand. The poem "helen of troy is asked to the spring formal" reimagines this parade of suitors as a pile of Tennessee boys, their golden tripods now field rests for rifles.

Homeric forms and techniques are used with intention in many poems in this book, including cataloguing in "helen of troy catalogues her pregnancy cravings" and the epic simile in "helen of troy meets the big cheese."

The golden shovel form—in which the last word of each line together recreates a quoted line or passage, used here in "helen of troy avoids her school reunion," "one more thing about the affair," and "helen of troy plants near the mailbox"—was created by the poet Terrance Hayes.

"helen of troy goes parking with the defensive tackle" rewrites the story of young Helen's rape and abduction by Theseus, a figure best known for slaying the half-bull, half-man Minotaur. In both myth and poem, Helen is eventually rescued by her brothers.

As a reward for proclaiming the goddess Aphrodite more beautiful than Hera or Athena, the Trojan prince Paris was promised Helen as his wife—although Helen had no say in the matter. The poem "helen of troy's turn to judge" places the outcome of the contest squarely in Helen's hands.

"the end of the affair" considers the inevitability of the fall of Troy and the carnage emerging from the belly of the Trojan Horse. In some stories, Helen circles the Trojan Horse while mimicking the voices of the hidden men's wives, whom they hadn't seen in a decade, enticing the men to reveal themselves and be slaughtered. In other stories, Helen lights a torch atop the city's tallest tower to signal to the hidden Greeks to emerge and begin their destruction.

About the Author

Maria Zoccola is a poet and educator from Memphis, Tennessee. She has writing degrees from Emory University and Falmouth University and has spent several years leading creative writing workshops for middle and high school youth. Maria's work has previously appeared in *Ploughshares*, *The Kenyon Review*, *The Iowa Review*, *The Sewanee Review*, *ZYZZYVA*, and elsewhere, and has received a special mention for the Pushcart Prize. *Helen of Troy, 1993* is her debut poetry collection.